CANCER, PRAYER AND SURVIVAL

Table of Contents

Introduction

This book is the story of the last thirty years of my life. It is certainly not a novel, neither would I consider it a short story. In one sense, it has a beginning, a middle but is still on-going. It is more a journal of a journey through cancer and beyond. It contains all the elements of life – pain, illness, disappointment, hope, even bewilderment. If any of these have touched your life, then read on. It might touch you or help with healing in some way, if only of bitterness or anger.

I see myself as a very ordinary run-of-the-mill person who has had an extraordinary experience that I wish to share. Because of what I have experienced, my story and how it brought me in touch with all my inner fears and insecurities may help someone else. A journey through cancer can be a harrowing experience to say the least.

Let me tell you a little about me, Mary. Born in 1952, I was reared in Walkinstown, Dublin. Both my parents were Civil Servants, both from Co Clare. I have an older brother and two younger sisters. It was the fifties, money was scarce, treats were rare but I have no recollection of feeling deprived in any way. We played on the road like everyone else, 'beds' – a version of hopscotch – skipping, chasing and sometimes on roller-skates. Of course girls helped their mammies and played with girls' toys, boys did no housework and played football on the green. Life was good, my health was good and everything was grand as far as I could see. I didn't particularly like school but I had no difficulty with learning. I read everything I could get my hands on and my younger sister Pauline and I spent a lot of time in Walkinstown library.

I loved day-dreaming and was highly imaginative. Of course in an imaginative situation I was always in charge. The 'fixer' in me was emerging even at an early age. My parents being from Clare, we had wonderful summer holidays 'down the country' in the days before foreign travel.

In my teenage years I was actually quite shy in a crowd, very unsure of myself. Like most teenagers I didn't like myself. What was the point in being good at school? I wanted to be good at sport, to have long blonde hair instead of my half-curly, wild dark brown hair. Nothing extraordinary here. I probably wasn't any different to any other teenager trying to grow up.

In the 60s I was mad into music. I was a big fan of Bob Dylan, Joan Baez and anyone really who was rebelling against the system. To me anyone who was singing about war , poverty or injustice of any kind was a hero and I too intended to do my bit to change the world. I also had this huge hunger to travel, to see places, to do things. I had this dream that when I got my first job, I was going to start saving immediately towards my first plane flight to anywhere.

As a Catholic born and bred, I always went to Mass, I suppose more out of habit than anything else. I said prayers for the usual things like passing exams and such. To be honest, I don't think I ever 'disbelieved'. God was there in the background to be called on in time of need. The rest of the time I presumed I was supposed to deal with things myself – 'Row in, make a muck of something, and then expect God to sort it out.' Never the other way round. I was an independent person who was well able to handle most situations.

I must say I was always a little in dread of the image of 'God the Father', a stern remote God. If you didn't go to Mass you might be struck by lightning or worse. Better to stay safe and keep the rules.

Emerging as a young adult, I qualified as a Primary teacher. At this stage I had had one fairly long relationship and one shorter, more intense one. At the age of 20, life was good. I had money for the first time in my life and I had been to France. You see? Some of my dreams were already panning out. I was in charge of my life and if you wanted something you could plan and save for it and it would happen. Again, the planner, fixer, in me was very much to the fore. You decided something, went after it and it would happen – or so I thought.

CHAPTER ONE

Stirrings of Spirituality

Around this time I was between boyfriends, on the loose you could say and a little fed up and bored. My best friend Mary, who was deeper into spirituality and certainly more adventurous along those lines than I was, got into TM, transcendental meditation. What deeper meaning was she looking for? Wasn't life good for the most part? I thought she was mad, off the wall as we say in Dublin.

She moved on to a prayer meeting in Eustace Street. The leader of that was a Pentecostal. The hall itself was a former Quaker hall. Every time we met, she seemed to be going on about these meetings and what good speakers they had. To me, a prayer meeting was for Baptists from the deep South of America. Sure didn't we have the Mass?

The fact is, Friday nights at the time were very boring. Do I stay in with the parents watching the *Late Late Show* or head to one of these meetings with Mary? What a choice. Making a conscious decision I wasn't going to be preached at, I found myself saying 'Oh alright, I'll go – just once maybe. Sure we can stay in town and head off for a few drinks afterwards.'

When we arrived, I must admit I had my guard up. I'm only here to support Mary; she's the one who wanted to come. I was also amazed at the number of people there, hundreds, the hall was packed and they were still coming in.

Then the singing started. These hymns were unlike any

I had heard at Mass – lively and joyful, full of praise and thanksgiving, with beautiful deep meaningful lyrics.

I always wrote poetry and enjoyed playing around with words. The lyrics of these songs to me were like wonderful poems. I was deeply impressed and, in spite of myself, touched, not so much by the sharings that night but by the music. I was always mad into music and would follow a good band or singer to the end of the earth. In retrospect, God, through my love of music, was drawing me closer, unknown to me, for the ordeals which were ahead and which were only round the corner.

At this stage I was around twenty-two years old and I had met the man I was going to marry. A crowd of us attended Eustace Street prayer meeting every Friday night, though I suspect Sean only came, some of the time anyhow, because I was going. Charismatic Renewal had arrived in Ireland. There was a great sense of excitement, of something new happening. For the first time ever, I was really listening to talks, some given by priests, some by lay people, some not even Catholic, and I was soaking up what they were saying.

The staid, slightly boring, slightly fearful church and it's attitude to God, with all it's rules and regulations, was being replaced with a totally different approach. There was more emphasis on the compassion of Jesus rather than the sterner more remote God the Father. I was avidly reading the Bible for the first time in my life, especially the New Testament. It was as if I was hearing the message that had always been there, for the very first time. As I recall, Catholics were not encouraged to read the Bible at all when I was growing up, in case we misinterpreted it or something. When I dug out my Bible from under a heap of old discarded school books, I found it almost brand new. We had to buy it, it was on the curriculum, but I have very little memory of ever referring to it or using it at all. Religion classes were a 'doss'. I think even the teacher must have been bored. None of them inspired me at any rate.

Friday nights became nearly the highlight of the week. I listened to the sharings and was amazed at the stories people had to tell, changed attitudes to life, healings even. We also 'adjourned' afterwards for a few drinks and often had very lively discussions about everything and anything – God, music, politics – nothing was barred. You could agree or disagree, good fun was had by all. We were all young and healthy and life was sweet.

I always enjoyed listening to a well-presented talk whether in a church, debating society or elsewhere. Some of the speakers in Eustace Street were particularly good – Fr Martin Tierney, Charles Lambe, Fr Chris O'Donnell, to name a few. It was around this time that we decided to move to a prayer meeting in Dublin Airport church as Fr Tierney was based there and led the meeting, on a Monday night. He also said Mass there once a month. The Mass was like an extended prayer meeting where people got up at an appointed time to share experiences, and the most solemn part, the consecration, was beautifully done and was so very special. I got a new sense of the presence of Jesus that I had never experienced before, but was to experience in an extraordinary sense a few short years later.

Imagine going the whole way to the airport on a Monday night on the bus, one into town and another out the north side. It made no sense but that is what we did. The prayer, the singing, the beautiful Masses that sometimes went on for two hours, the people we met, the friends we made. Yes, life was truly for living and everything was wonderful.

We were planning to marry at this stage, and were saving hard for a house. We both had a very positive attitude towards life. We deserved a house if we put our back into saving for one. If you worked hard, didn't you deserve the end result?

Well, we did get married and a great day was had by all. We bought our house and were enjoying the usual things, painting, planning furniture etc. It was an exciting time. What we were about to find out was that this grand happy, healthy life that we somehow felt we deserved was about to change radically, never to be the same again. We discovered that you have no power at all over the major events in your life. Our lovely bubble of safety and happiness was about to burst. We were about to embark on a journey full of sickness and heartache that was to affect every aspect of our life together.

This is how it began.

CHAPTER TWO

The shocking news of the big C

We married on 2 April 1977. I was 24 and Sean was 22. After our honeymoon we were both back at work and within about six weeks I was pregnant. Although it happened very quickly, we were both thrilled and excited. Now we didn't just have a house. We were looking forward to setting up a home where we would raise our own family.

In June of that year some of our friends in Renewal wanted to head to Ann Arbour in Michigan, USA to experience prayer groups and community living over there. Lots of people were going and as many as possible were encouraged to go, ourselves included. The long and the short of it is, off we went, full of curiosity, leaving our new house without a stick of furniture except for a bed and two second-hand armchairs. Luckily, Sean, being a carpenter, had fitted a kitchen himself.

My first impression of the States was the relentless heat and the humidity and pretending to be enjoying myself when I wasn't really feeling well at all. As far as I remember we were 22 days in America and I just began to feel sicker and sicker. To me, there were too many talks to go to, too many prayer meetings, or maybe I felt so rotten I just wanted to go home. The whole experience was too much for me. I just felt so drained all the time. I was so weak on the way home I actually spent some time on the floor of the plane.

Of course, people had been telling me, 'I was like that on my first. You'll be grand after the first three months, etc.' I had actually attended a hospital in the States as we were down visiting relations of Sean's on the way home. They did a blood test and were anxious to admit me then and there, without actually telling us anything. 'Further tests,' they said. I flatly refused, conscious of the cost of healthcare in America, and insisted on leaving. They then gave me a letter for my doctor and told me to contact him immediately when I got home. This we did. He took one look at the letter and sent for an ambulance to take me to Holles Street Hospital, where I was booked in to have my baby. He said it was just to be safe, to check things out. Nobody had as yet told us anything alarming.

When writing this, I checked with Sean how long I was in Holles Street, as to me it was just a few hours. Apparently it was days rather than hours. That will give you some idea of my mental and physical state at the time. I didn't know day from night. I lost all interest in eating. It was as if someone had pulled a cork and all of my life's blood was draining out of me, taking my energy with it. To open my eyes, to focus on what people were asking me or saying to me was all too much. I just wanted everyone to go away and leave me alone.

I think it may have been in Holles Street that I was anointed for the first time. I have vague memories of a very young priest asking me if I wanted to confess anything. I had no interest at all, nor could I join in even a simple prayer. It was too much effort to try to remember any-thing. There were candles lit on the table at the end of the bed but I know for a fact it still had not occurred to me that I might be dying. I didn't care, I was too tired to care, why wouldn't he just go away? Apparently, I was told after-wards, I asked him to come back next week!

A few days later, I was transferred to St Vincent's hospital in Elm Park, which over the next four years was to become nearly a 'home from home'. I arrived there in July and for the following three months I never even put my foot on the floor, let alone go home. When Sean went to meet the Consultant, he was on his own. Without waiting until some of his family or mine were there to support him, he was told I had leukemia (Acute Lymphatic). I was in a bad way, the prognosis was not good. They would try their best to keep me alive until the baby was viable but there was no hope at all for me.

Sean was 23 years old, we were three months married and his wife was dying.

At this stage, I wasn't told anything and, to be honest, I was too sick to care. Even though I was pregnant they began chemotherapy. Now, because I have dreadful, small thready veins and the treatment was intravenous, the next few months were a total nightmare, for them as well as for me. For them, drips constantly breaking down, veins thrombosed, and the frustration of looking for another vein sometimes at three in the morning. For me, jabs, more jabs, 'sorry, we'll try again', black and blue all over – sometimes still no success. I saw doctors going off for a break before coming back to try again. I'd say there are doctors out there who still remember my veins! To this day many years later the vein from my left wrist to my elbow is still rock hard. It never recovered fully and at one stage my left arm would not straighten. I stayed in that bed from July to the end of September without a break and a lot of it is a haze of pain, discomfort and vomiting, or trying to. They allowed me home towards the end of September for my first break from the hospital. I came home on a Friday, got a dreadful nose bleed on the Sunday morning which wouldn't stop. With my nose pouring like a tap I had to head back to the hospital where I was admitted straight away. The next few months were a constant round of chemotherapy sessions, short trips home, supposedly for three weeks, rarely lasting that long because of a plague of infections which seemed never-ending. My hair had fallen out in clumps with the chemotherapy sessions, though not completely.

Up to this stage the baby was still alive, growing and thriving even though I wasn't. I think the only reason I sat up and tried to eat most days was for the baby's sake. I myself had neither the interest nor the energy to be bothered. My weight was dropping dramatically. I remember looking in the mirror one morning and remarking that I looked like one of the famine victims in Biafra. I was skin and bone. From a weight of eight and a half stone on my wedding day I was down now to six and a half stone. Did I care? I don't think so. All my energy went into dragging myself from one day to the next.

CHAPTER THREE

News of the baby

Was God in the picture at this stage? I know all of our friends and relations were storming heaven night and day. The airport prayer group apparently met early every Monday night to pray especially for me. I don't think I myself said many prayers, formal or otherwise in those days. Sometimes I tried, but couldn't remember the words, so I gave up. But as anyone who was ever in hospital knows, the days are very long and I know I often had little conversations with Jesus as a friend, as a confidante. 'Jesus, tell them to go away … Please keep the drip working … Help me to swallow some food … Help me to keep it down … Help me to sleep' – very basic needs. Sometimes I noticed a little prayer answered, especially if I got a whole night's uninterrupted sleep, no need to re-site the drip. I began to be thankful for small things, to live in the immediate.

People were coming in to visit all the time and sometimes I would feel so buoyed up by a good laugh or a word of encouragement. I don't remember asking to get better at this stage. I was just about able to get from hour to hour. I went from breakfast to bedbath to doctors floating in and out, to visitors, to medication, to sleep, without ever putting my feet on the floor. I know I asked Jesus to stay close, especially if I was being wheeled down for a test. Every so often they did a lumbar puncture or a bone marrow test. The first lumbar puncture I ever had, I temporarily lost all feeling from the waist down, which terrified the wits out of me. So the next time one of those was scheduled, you can imagine how I felt. I prayed and prayed for Jesus to stay very close, to guide their hands. I sweated bricks. I got a mental picture of Jesus sweating blood in the Garden of Gethsemane. He too was terrified of what he knew was ahead. He wasn't sure if he could go ahead with it and his friends deserted him and fell asleep. I could talk to him about fear. He would understand. He, as a human, had experienced it. When I was wheeled down for the second lumbar puncture, I felt much calmer. Everything went smoothly this time. I was very thankful for that mental image. I had learnt a new thing. It was okay to be afraid and Jesus had been there with me. All had gone well.

At this stage my energy levels were climbing a little, mentally and physically, and I began keeping a diary, journalling again, which became a life-saver over the years. I dipped into a little *New Testament and Psalms* that I kept beside the bed and when I couldn't think of a prayer I read a psalm – some of them are beautiful prayers. If ever I was a bit down or just couldn't understand why all of this was happening, I wrote down how I felt. Before you write something down, you have to think it out first. Sometimes it helped to clarify things or at least to look at it from a different angle. Often I got a helpful word from a reading or a poem or some other source.

I think writing helped me to focus on now, today, as I was usually writing in the evening, reflecting on the good and not so good parts of the day, trying to be positive about little things that went well and trying to cope with other things that didn't. I didn't think much about the following day. There was no point in worrying about things that might happen tomorrow. I had enough to cope with as it was. I was learning unknown to myself that you do actually get the grace and strength for now, no more.

Around this time, as a couple, we got to the very lowest

point in our life together. As I said, the baby was growing well and I was spending a little longer at home between chemo sessions, usually about three weeks, when my legs began to swell really badly. I attended Holles Street for my check-up, trusting they would sort me out. I was told there was nothing much to worry about. Back I went to Vincent's for more chemo, where I could read the concern, alarm even, in their faces. I was transferred immediately back to Holles Street with them mumbling something about a possible problem they wanted checked out. No-one told us anything. The doctor came in and I was brought down for a scan. I suspected something was up but no-one would answer any questions. I was brought back to my room by a very silent, business-like nurse who assured me the doctor would be up shortly. A cup of tea was brought and I was left on my own. Next thing, in comes the doctor and announces bluntly, 'Your baby is dead Mrs. We can't get a heartbeat', just like that! I was so stunned, I don't think I could think of a single thing to say or ask about. Sean arrived and we just sat there. I don't think I fully believed what I had heard. It just didn't sink in.

Nobody appeared for a while, then in breezed another doctor asking us things like, 'Would you like to continue to full term or have the baby induced?' I was thirty-one weeks pregnant. How could I possibly make a decision like that at that moment in time? We were still shattered by the first news. He left and said he would return later. We were offered no counseling, no support or even a leaflet, just asked to make a decision as soon as we could.

I didn't think I could go another nine weeks knowing I was carrying a dead baby. It was that that finally helped me to decide to go for the induction. I went to bed, and Sean went home eventually. We were both on our own that night trying to cope with this latest blow. Things were to get worse.

The following morning, Sean arrived in, looking shattered. I knew there was something else I wasn't being told. He looked very uncomfortable. He finally told me that my father had died the night before, quite suddenly. I knew he had been ill and that my poor mother had been commuting between the Adelaide Hospital and Vincent's everyday day for months, but I hadn't been told he was that bad, or they possibly didn't want to worry me. So within twenty-four hours, I had to cope with the news that both my father and baby were dead.

CHAPTER FOUR

Funeral, deaths of my father and the baby

How did I get through the days that followed? I think I was in such shock that I floated through it. It was all so sudden, so unreal. I don't remember 'feeling' as such. Since I was in Holles Street at the time, I asked permission to go out for my father's funeral. It was decided that I could, but they also wanted to discuss what I wanted to do about the baby. My own gut feeling was that I would go ahead with the induction. I didn't think I had the courage or the inner strength to keep going to full term. There was just too much going on, too much grief and shock. To be honest, I don't think I really absorbed the implications of what they were talking about or the effect it might have on me. They allowed me out to attend the funeral Mass but I was to report straight back in to be induced the following morning.

I left the hospital with Sean and we headed for Walkinstown. I knew there was no way I could bring my mother up to date on my news just then. I had to be strong for her. So I carried my dark terrible secret to the church, shook hand with relations and went through all the motions. People were actually consoling me saying things like 'God takes one life but gives another', referring to my very obvious bump, no-one knowing except me that there was no other life. I said goodbye to my mam, and watched the hearse leaving the church for Co Clare where my dad was to be buried. It was to be a while before I got back to visit the grave. I had to ask which graveyard he was in, as people forgot I wasn't there for the funeral.

Sean's brother and his wife brought us for lunch and everyone was very kind and caring. At this stage we had told a few people about the baby but there was little anyone could do. Eventually we had to head back to Holles Street to face the inevitable. Sean stayed as long as he could but the time came for him to leave too and I found myself in a very lonely, frightening place with the whole night ahead of me and little else to think about except what was to happen the next day.

The morning came, and was terrifying in many respects. Firstly, I was preparing for a birth never having attended even one pre-natal class, as most of the time up to this I had been in Vincent's Hospital, only visiting the maternity hospital for the odd check-up. In breezed this doctor and connected me up to a drip, whistling away to himself. He was about to leave when I had to ask him, 'What is going to happen next?' How would I know if anything was happening, etc.? All he said was that a nurse would be along soon to fill me in and promptly left the room, leaving me there on my own without the faintest idea what was going to happen or when.

After a while a nurse did appear and kindly filled me in a little. I went into labour quite quickly but it was very long and drawn out. Sean was in the hospital but was not allowed to accompany me to the delivery room. Thirteen hours later I was delivered of a baby girl. She weighed just over a kilogramme. She was dead and I was exhausted.

To this day, thirty years later, I have never forgotten that moment. The silence in the delivery room was weird, eerie, no new-born cry, just a horrible deathly silence. The nurses busied themselves, avoiding eye-contact at all times. My little daughter was bundled up and whisked off. I had to ask if it was a boy or a girl. I asked if I could see her or hold her and was told that wouldn't be a good idea and off she went out the door. I never saw my baby and have neither a lock of her hair or a photograph to remember her by. I have never had a moment so dark, so bleak in my life.

Sean didn't appear for a while – they wouldn't let him in for the birth. He told me that while he was waiting outside, a man got the joyous news that his wife was safely delivered – twins! Sean knew we were going to have nothing. While I was delivering the baby, how empty and lonely he must have felt in that waiting room. Remember he was trying to be strong for me. This was the lowest point in our lives to date. It was the ninth of November 1977.

We left the hospital probably the next day but not only had we no little bundle, we couldn't even go home to our own house as I had to report back to Vincent's Hospital. We were both feeling very low.

We went back in towards town. I didn't want to go back to the hospital immediately. We needed a bit of time together, a bit of space. God knows we had little of that with me in hospital so much. We headed into the Kilkenny Design Centre for a bit of lunch where I have no memory of either of us eating anything.

The hospital had asked us at the time, a few hours after the birth, if we wanted them to bury the baby or arrange a private funeral. 'We called her Mary after you,' they said. I think I was in such a state at that stage, I didn't feel up to arranging a funeral. There wasn't time anyway as I was due to be re-admitted to Vincent's. We decided to allow them to bury her.

So in a way, there was no grief, no funeral, no memories of what she looked like, nothing in fact to hang on to at all. We didn't baptise her or even give her the name we had planned for her. There was to be no closure for another twenty years, which I will share in a later chapter.

I went back to Vincent's, Sean eventually went home

and back to work and life such as it was went on. As it happened, there was little time for anything to sink in or time for tears, as I was only a few weeks in the hospital when my appendix began to give trouble and before I knew it, I was back on the operating table. So much was going on, I think I went into shock on a semi-permanent basis!

Was I angry? I don't think it even occurred to me at the time. Was I upset, tearful? Yes. Was I mystified or puzzled? I suppose I was. Did I blame God or anyone else for that matter? I don't think so. I was too busy recovering from one shock and coping with the next one.

I did know that the airport prayer group were still faithfully praying every Monday night. I myself had definitely given up formal prayer at this stage. I had moved on to conversations with Jesus, sometimes giving out loads, other times too sick, too lacking in energy. Other times just being still, very quiet, not bothering much with words – in a way I was learning to be reflective unknown to myself.

These were often the best times, as Jesus could get a word in now that I had shut up! I was learning to just 'be' and it was good, no trying to organise or fix anything, doing nothing – most unlike me!

At this stage, remember, I was supposed to be near death. The original prognosis was that I would be dead by Christmas and it was now early December. Luckily, I was blissfully unaware of this but it must have been very much on other peoples' minds, especially Sean's.

Looking back now on that time, I can see how I was changing in little ways. Gone was the 'Mary who planned ahead, who organised things'. I had been stripped of all power over what might happen next and could make no decisions even as to when they would allow me home for a break. I couldn't fix anything anymore. I wasn't even sure if I could keep my breakfast down. I was growing out of a dependence on me, for everything, and into more of a dependence on God to get me through the day. What am I talking about? – to get me through the next hour would be nearer the truth.

Because the day in hospital seems very long sometimes, and you're bed-bound a lot of the time with very little energy, I found myself reflecting a lot or quietly day-dreaming. Sometimes when visitors arrived and I was feeling a bit low, I found something they said would be exactly what I needed to hear. I think this was Jesus' way of talking to me, comforting me, reassuring me. I saw these people as guardian angels sent with a message, unknown to themselves. I think I was starting to notice how near God was, just through a kind word or a smile.

I kept a writing pad on my locker and sometimes wrote down what people said, or took a lovely phrase or a poem from a get well card. Later in the quiet of the night-time I would read them. I had a small *New Testament and Psalms* and I would read a psalm now and again. I kept a little diary of my thoughts – I suppose a form of journalling. I sometimes wrote a poem. It all helped to preserve my sanity and gave me a sense of peace. I found it easier to lie down and sleep. It became easier to leave things I couldn't fix and stop worrying about the next day. I started to say this little prayer:

Now I lay me down to sleep,
for in you alone, Lord,
I lay down in safety.

Right up to the present day, I say it last thing every night.

I actually managed to get home for Christmas that year and got back to work in January. I had a wonderful

Principal who must have been in touch with the Almighty because I actually managed to get through a whole term at school without missing a day. That's the wonderful thing about young children, they demand your full attention, leaving you no time at all to think of yourself or your problems – very therapeutic for me. I was still having chemotherapy sessions but the treatment was more spread out now, once every three months or so. And lo and behold, in spite of all the odds, I was still alive.

CHAPTER FIVE

Learning the truth

Thus began 1978, and to me, if not to everyone else, I was getting better. I could cope with school, I seemed to be avoiding infections, and most important of all for me, I was out of hospital. I suppose I thought this nightmare was now behind me and I could get on with my life. I had a few drinks at the weekend, went shopping, had a laugh, things were returning to normal, but it wasn't to be.

Around Easter time I began to feel quite unwell again. I was very bloated and had lost my appetite. I returned to hospital for a chemo session and they discovered I had developed adhesions from the appendix operation. The inside of the wound hadn't healed properly, possibly because I wasn't in the best of health. I was told another operation was on the cards and before I knew it I was back 'on the table'.

I know at the time I was very disappointed. I had just clapped myself on the back that I had completed a full term at school and was looking forward to the summer term. It seemed that all plans had to be put on hold again and, frustrated as I was, there was nothing for it but to accept it.

Around this time, I began to really question what was going on and why God seemed to be 'picking on me'. I prayed everyday that God would give me a break. In retrospect, I was praying for the wrong thing altogether. I realised one day that all my petitions were focused on *me* and what *I* wanted. 'Please God make me well so that I can get back to work, so that I can start living again.' None of these prayers were giving me any peace. Then one day, I read one of the psalms: 'Blessed be God because he has not rejected my prayer or removed his love from me.' It was the second part that struck me. Here I was, screaming at God and he was reminding me that he was there with me every step of the way, loving, strengthening, gracing every hour. It never said anything in the Old or New Testaments that I have read that following Jesus was going to be a piece of cake. He never said it would be easy. He *did* promise he would never leave us alone.

That day was a bit of a revelation for me. Instead of asking and even pleading with him, I decided to let Jesus decide when the right time would be for me to resume work and living in general. Instead, I spent a while getting in touch with my fears and anxieties, pouring out my soul, admitting my frustration, bawling for a while but finally coming to the conclusion that no matter what happened tomorrow, I would be safe. God would be very near. I calmed way down and allowed his peace to creep into the depths of my soul.

From then on, I stopped wishing and wanting and dreaming, and accepted where I was at that point in time. I think it was St Paul who said, 'Whatever state I am in, I have learned to be content.' To get the grace to know and really believe that we're not on our own, I think, is one of the most valuable lessons I have ever learned. The second most important thing is to know that you are loved, that you are really very special to God.

We all know that the love of a parent is very special. Even though their child might stray or get into trouble, or disappoint, or even shock, I don't think it interferes with the love that's there. In a very subtle way, Jesus was putting these thoughts in my head and like a typical teenager, sometimes I was listening and sometimes I wasn't. If you think about it, how many teenagers listen to their parents? But doesn't the parent always love, always worry, always hope that the child will come round in the end and do well?

I remember lying in the bed one day and getting a very clear picture of a maze. I, of course, was floundering around in the middle of it and God was looking down. He could see the whole picture from his angle. 'Take the next left', he was saying. 'Don't be ridiculous,' I was saying, 'there's nothing round that corner only weeds.' On it went, God doing his best to guide me to where I should be and me of course being headstrong and stupid. That image gave me a very clear lesson on the times when I choose, very selectively, to listen to God's wisdom or follow my own plan. He is trying to show me how to cope with the day, but I would like it to be different.

Well, I left hospital eventually after the adhesions operation and do you know what? Within a few weeks I had totally cast aside any shreds of wisdom I had learned and had 'reverted to normal'. I was talking to Jesus every day, thanking him for how well I was doing but not listening to a word he was saying.

At this stage, you've probably guessed, the next bombshell was just around the corner. Back from a chemo session, the doctor announced very casually, that it was now time for radiotherapy. You have to remember that up to this point, I still thought I had some form of anaemia. All this 'treatment', which I had never been told was chemo, was to help me to regain my health and get well. Nobody in the hospital or at home had ever mentioned the word 'Cancer'. I suppose the doctor presumed I had been told by Sean or a member of my family, but I hadn't. Maybe when they saw me pass the Christmas deadline, they were hoping they might never have to, I don't know. All I do know is that I got some shock and was hugely angry with everyone for stringing me along. Who did they think they were? How dare they make that decision? For a few hours I wasn't talking to anyone. I wanted to be on my own and in no uncertain terms, told them all to go away.

'So that's it now, Lord,' I remember saying, 'All this time and I'm going to die anyway.'

My first reaction was anger. My next was to grab a piece of paper and make a list of things I wanted to do. I had to leave my affairs in order, didn't I? There were private diaries to be burnt, personal things I would want people to have, people I needed to talk to, etc. I remember going into a frenzy of activity for a few hours, of course blocking out the stark reality of what I now had to contend with. Cancer. I was going to die.

After a few hours, exhausted from all my planning, I fell asleep. When I woke up, an extraordinary peace had replaced all the activity and, when the doctor came in, I was able to tell him to go ahead and book me in for the radiotherapy. I was able to ask him some rational questions – how many sessions, possible side effects, etc. It was then I was told that my hair, that had fallen out in clumps with the chemo, was now going to fall out completely with this treatment. I remember asking the ridiculous question – will it hurt? Is it painful? Being reassured that it wouldn't, I decided that it didn't sound that bad. After all, chemo sessions were intravenous and after the battering my veins had been through, anything that didn't involve drips sounded okay to me.

CHAPTER SIX

Being bald

So now I had to contend with this latest news – twelve sessions of radiotherapy and when it is finished, you won't have a blade of hair left on your head. I'm not sure which news was more overwhelming, the fact that I had to have this treatment because I had cancer, or how I would cope with baldness.

They decided to keep me in hospital for the duration of the treatment. They said it would be easier to monitor me and that I might be very nauseous. Every day I would be transferred to St Anne's in Northbrook Road by ambulance and brought back to Vincent's afterwards.

The evening before I was to start I was sitting on the bed in the hospital trying to cope with a huge range of emotions. One, believe it or not, was relief. I had been puzzled for a while as to why I was still receiving treatment for what I thought was anaemia. I was wondering why I was not getting better. No one had ever mentioned the word chemotherapy to me. Now everything was out in the open. I could talk about it now with Sean which made it easier for him. At least he didn't have to pretend anymore that all would be well. I found myself able to say the word Leukemia, to confront it, let the idea sink in, discuss it with friends, cry about it.

The next emotion that evening was fear. An overwhelming fear of vulnerability, for want of a better word – a complete loss of control over everything. This was going to happen whether I liked it or not and there was absolutely nothing I could do to stop it.

Well, the next morning, off I went in the ambulance, having washed and brushed my thick dark brown hair as I thought possibly for the last time. True to their word there was no pain – a lot of anxiety lying there for a few minutes, my eyes covered with lead, but there was no pain. I was also waiting for the nausea, which thankfully didn't come.

The days passed, I still had my hair, and I still had no nausea. I spent every evening for at least a half-hour if not longer praying that I wouldn't lose my hair. 'Ask and you will receive' etc. I really hoped and believed that Jesus would hear my prayer. I think I was terrified of the notion of baldness. Well, I got to the end of the treatment, my hair still intact and headed for home, thanking Jesus all the way. See, he does hear and answer!

A few days later, Sean was gone to work and I was pottering around the bedroom tidying up. I got a strong urge to stop what I was doing, sit down and have my special time. I thanked God over and over for all he had done and was really feeling very up-beat and special. I opened my wee book intending to read a psalm, to give thanks. The thing was, every reading I got was about 'letting go', about pride, about fear. It dawned on me that my prayer was wrong again. It was all about what *I* wanted. What would people think if they saw me bald? I'd have to cover up going out in public, me that never wore a hat and loved to feel the breeze blowing through my hair. I'd never cope with a wig.

I suppose I had the stupid notion that people would be embarrassed, that Sean wouldn't love me anymore. I was not the girl he married now. I was less than seven stone in weight. I was a skinny, bald, unattractive wife. Fear was there all the time about so many things. That's why I wanted God to 'fix' it. It became hugely clear in a very few minutes that I should have been asking Jesus to help me deal with the fear, this terrible fear that I mightn't be loved as much without my hair. So I found myself changing my prayer. I got a reading, 'God loves you with a love beyond all telling' and another, 'I will not leave you orphaned.' He was telling me to let go of the fear and it would be okay. So I prayed for the grace to do that. I felt a great peace and imagined myself 'parcelling up' my fear and handing it over. Then I got up, went over to the dressing-table and brushed my hair. Every last blade fell to the floor. It was as if he waited until I was ready. I was now completely bald. I looked into the mirror and realised I didn't look that bad. In fact I didn't really give a damn and went off down the stairs feeling quite light-hearted.

After that, for a while, I wore this awful wig in public which felt as tight as a bathing cap. I hated it with a vengeance. It gave me headaches. I ditched it very soon afterwards and bought a load of cheap scarves, different ones to suit different jumpers. Sean had reassured me that he still loved me, so all was well.

I realised what a terrible thing fear can be, especially if you're sitting at home letting it get in on you and sharing it with no-one. Because I scribble and journal a lot – one of my ways of coping and trying to make sense of things – I wrote a poem during this time. I think I'll say no more on the subject; the poem says it all.

Fear
Two paths unfolding
Lying ahead
On which one to venture
Full of dread
Do I follow that signpost
Leading to fear
Of pain, blood

Many a tear?
This fear of the future
And what it might hold
I could dwell on forever
If I let it unfold
I could sense with foreboding
The ominous clouds
Gripping, consuming me
Screaming out loud
Slowly wrecking
Disturbing my soul
So useless, this fear
Just making me old
I'll take to the other path
Eyes closed, I'll jump in
I'll abandon my fear
And trust fully in him
I'll soar way beyond
Fear of pain and sorrow
And put all my trust in him
For tomorrow

Admittedly, this is no brilliant reflection, nor is there any great depth in it, but it does give you an idea of where I was at at the time – a silly rhyme to some, a great release for me.

CHAPTER SEVEN

News of Infertility

Well, I got back on my feet once more and life went on. We had a nice summer, uncomplicated by set-backs or illness, some of it spent in Co Clare, some in Dublin and a lovely holiday on Achill Island. I think, at this stage I was constantly on the look out for the next 'blip' and got a little paranoid about being near people who had coughs or colds, but as the summer went on, I got stronger and more confident. I appeared to be staying well and free of infection.

Back to school I went in September and very gradually eased my way into a semblance of normality. I had enough hair now to visit a hairdresser and get a bit of a shape on it, which I did. Even though it was still very short, I ditched the scarves and walked around feeling whole again for the first time in ages. Thank God life was good. I was still alive and determined to live it to the full. I was still having chemo sessions, though very spread out now and check-ups every week for blood tests. I was staying in remission, I was feeling very well and my doctor told me he was 'gobsmacked'. His words were, 'When I look at you I close the books.' But being a doctor and a man of science, he was very cautious. I wasn't finished with chemo sessions just yet and he would keep a very close eye on me!

The rest of 1978 and all the way through 1979, I stayed very well and fairly infection-free. Life was very good and I grabbed it by the throat.

In the hospital, I had got into the habit of 'being still',

rather than gossiping away to God. I kept this up and found that my prayer now was very different. I was still, I was quiet, I was listening and I discovered, if you like, a different Jesus. It was like a lovely relationship, a friendship that grew and grew. I was drawn every day to make sure I found time for this 'stillness' and I must say I thrived on it. Sometimes a thought or word or even an image would come into my head and often it would be just what I needed to hear for that day – guidance if you like, sometimes comfort, sometimes a little 'pearl of wisdom'. Unknown to myself, I was being brought along by the hand, being taught by the Master himself. I didn't just believe anymore. It was deeper than that. I just *knew* there was a loving God and if I gave him the time, I could really come into his presence. Sometimes, I got no word or even an idea at all, but I soaked up the peace of the whole experience. It became my special time and as time went on I found I couldn't do without it.

Yes, 1979 was a good year for us. Of course we went to the Phoenix Park to see the Pope along with half a million others. What a day that was – crowds and crowds of people, everyone with 'pope's chairs' and picnics, everyone helping everyone else. I remember I was so delighted with myself because I didn't need any help. I don't think I even sat down!

Soon after that, we were talking and wondering if maybe I was well enough to try for another baby. I was due for a check-up as usual. Sean came along and we decided to ask. Because it was just a check-up, I just took the morning off work, as did Sean. I was due back at school by lunchtime. We did ask and the news we got shook me to the core. We were very gently and tactfully told that because of all the chemo I had had, and wasn't finished yet, the surest side effect of that was infertility – I would not be having any more babies. I just sat there, numb. Sean didn't appear that shocked. Maybe he had an inkling or something, but I just sat there and stared. I couldn't or wouldn't believe what I just heard. Of course, the doctor was saying things like, 'There is life beyond children … Aren't you lucky to be still alive?' etc. But I took none of it in. We had lost the little baby we had and there were to be no others. There were no words to describe how I felt, none at all.

We left the hospital and all I could think of was, how on earth could I go back to school, but I had said I would be back by lunchtime and felt I couldn't let people down. So I packed Sean back to work, assuring him I could cope and walked in the school gates to my classroom, where the children were just heading out to play. I listened to their little stories, I smiled at their jokes, I finished out the day. The mothers with all their little babies and toddlers came to collect their children. I was totally without feeling, dead even to pain or grief.

My principal happened to ask me how I had got on in the hospital and, in a dead-pan voice, I just trotted out the news. She just took one look at me and the state I was in and marched me over to the convent. She was quite an austere nun herself though very fair and kind, and I remember thinking what on earth she was going to say. Maybe give me a talk on the will of God? I decided it didn't matter, nothing she could say would make any difference. She sat me down in the polished parlour and disappeared. The door opened and back she came with a glass of brandy! I had underestimated this woman – she knew words were no use so she didn't bother using any. I eventually got home and mechanically made the dinner. I don't think I cried very much. I know I had a pain in my gut that lasted for days. I was mystified. What was going on? Why another blow now? I remembered the story of the man who clawed his way to the top of the mountain. Battered and exhausted he reached the top. Had he a feeling of triumph, of exhilaration? No. What did he see in front of him but another mountain, even bigger and more dangerous-looking than the first. Is this what life was going to be like for us? Were we never going to get a break?

I was having my special time every day but mostly I was too numb to allow God to get through. Usually I just sat there and I don't think I wanted to know what Jesus had to say. I was physically well but I was dying inside. I was totally browned off with one blow after another. What Jesus did in those dark days was not to try to fill me with words of wisdom or consolation – I wouldn't have listened anyway – but in a totally practical way, people turned up that I could talk to. A nurse in the hospital told me she knew of someone who had had chemo and now had children. Whether this was true or not didn't matter to me. What I needed was hope and I grabbed every shred of it when the opportunity presented itself. If you haven't got hope, you have nothing.

Time passed and very, very slowly I began to accept that we wouldn't have children. We still had each other and I seemed to be staying well. We really did have a lot to be thankful for. We started to do up our own house and got involved in sorting out the garden. We planned for weekends away and in our own way generally got on with things. People, supposedly helping, suggested things like, 'Why don't you get a cat?' There's one thing sure, you have no control over what people will say and they probably mean it for the best.

I found school hugely helpful during this time. Young children demand your full attention and you don't have a minute to call your own. This proved to be very good for me. There were schemes to plan, songs to be taught, etc. I had no time at all to feel sorry for myself or to mope. So Jesus was there, was looking after my needs. I had a job I loved and could throw myself into and a loving husband who was dealing with his grief, our grief in his own way. We had had illness and tragedy but we were still together and there for each other. After another while, I found that the pain in my gut, or heart, was beginning to ease until the day came when I was able to 'parcel it up' and hand it over. I was able to say that it's okay if we don't have any children. I could accept that we wouldn't have and I had a new peace about the whole thing. I could laugh and enjoy a joke again. I could go out and enjoy a bit of fun. I still hadn't got to the stage of genuinely admiring a newborn baby, but I knew it would come in time.

CHAPTER EIGHT

Healing and birth

One day in 1980, it must have been a Saturday as Sean was home, and again we were working on the garden which was still very neglected. At one stage we had a thistle all of six feet tall in the back garden. Sean was working away with a scythe and I decided to stroll up to the shops for a paper. It was 10 o'clock in the morning and as Mass was just starting I decided to head into the church. Everything was normal. I nodded at a few neighbours and didn't notice anything in particular about the readings. When the time came to receive the Eucharist, up I went. It was then that the most extraordinary thing happened. I was back in my seat and beginning my prayers. Suddenly, I felt an overwhelming sense of peace or love or something I couldn't quite put my finger on. For a few seconds it was like being transported to somewhere else, though I had no vision. I felt so wonderful and wanted it to go on and on. But it didn't. I 'came to' as it were and found myself still kneeling in my seat, with the priest saying the final prayers. I knew a wonderful healing or blessing had taken place and I suppose I had a huge sense of having been touched very specially. It's as if I had experienced a few seconds in the very presence of God in a way I had never experienced before, or since for that matter. It was powerful and wonderful. I knew deep down, without any nod or indication from a priest or a doctor, that I was going to be okay. I had a great sense that this was a very important part of my healing, the restoration of my fertility and the amazing part was I hadn't been praying for that at all!

I began to menstruate very slightly there in the church, which hadn't happened for months and very infrequently for a year or two before that. I knew, from that moment, without a doubt, we were going to have another child fairly soon or sometime in the future. I was touched very specially that morning and one day, in God's own time I was going to be completely healed.

Armed with this newly acquired wisdom, and literally glowing with excitement, I raced down the hill and in home. I burst into the house and launched into my news – that I was going to be healed and we were going to have babies and everything. Sean took one incredulous look at me, thought I had lost the run of myself, and asked me to put the kettle on.

Well, nothing further happened for a few months, the garden got sorted and life settled down again. For me, though, life would never be the same again. I blabbed to all my friends, especially those in Renewal, about my experience but I don't think any of them really believed me. I was on my own with this, but I didn't care. It was as if Jesus and I had a secret which would come out in due course.

And out it did come when in October 1980, I suspected I might be pregnant. I hoped and prayed for it to be true, but being human I suppose, I was terrified to check it out. Here I was, thanking God for my healing and at the same time not fully trusting that it might be true. I began to have doubts – it's wishful thinking, a phantom pregnancy. Then I remembered that morning in the church and all the readings I ever had about Jesus and the crowds, 'laying his hands on them he healed them'.

Did he lay his hands on me that morning? And if he

did, why do I still doubt? A terrible fear came over me. Could I handle another disappointment? Would people laugh or feel sorry for me? For the next few days I had mixed feelings until it finally dawned on me that all these doubts had no place in my heart. I either believed or I didn't. So did I? I knew the answer to that. Along I went for a pregnancy test, thanking God all the way for this new little baby that was now growing inside me, constantly re-minding myself that nothing was impossible with God. 'Congratulations,' the doctor said, 'Your baby is due in mid-June and all seems in order at the moment.'

I must say, in one sense I felt exhilarated and excited, and in another sense I felt ashamed. God had given me such a direct sign and I thought I really believed and yet, when push came to shove, I had doubted, I hadn't trusted, I had been afraid. Now, in spite of all my human frailties and short-comings, God still chose to heal me. My fertility was fully restored. We were expecting a baby in spite of all the odds. You have to remember I was still having regular chemotherapy sessions. Sean, I think, was thrilled at the news if a little speechless and apprehensive.

After all, it had come up in conversation with the doc-tor at one stage that for someone in my precarious state of health to get pregnant, which I wouldn't of course, my im-mune system would have to drop to accept the baby. If my immune system dropped any further, I wouldn't survive the pregnancy. Such was the prognosis at the time.

Reminded of this, I wondered what I would tell my consultant. Did he believe in God or miracles? Would he blame us? How stupid were we to be taking chances! What chances? Why would we be taking precautions when we were told there would be no more children? Were we not supposed to be relating as a married couple? I wasn't due back for a blood test for a week or two and I was caught between bursting to tell him the good news and wondering how he would receive it. I took the coward's way out. I wrote to him so he would be prepared when we met!

Along came my check-up date and out I went to the hospital. First he had been 'gobsmacked' that I had recovered at all, now he was amazed again that something they had never expected in a million years had occurred. He ranted on a bit about us taking chances, which I knew he would. Then he began to look terribly worried and explained again about the huge risk to my own life carrying this child. I would also have to put the rest of my chemotherapy sessions on hold for the duration of the pregnancy, a fact with which he was not at all comfortable.

I must say, I never felt more peaceful or relaxed than I did that day, and it ended up with me assuring him everything would be fine!

The pregnancy progressed without a hitch, with me blooming and not even a cough or cold in sight. I think for every pound I gained, Sean lost one! He was climbing the walls watching my every move after what the doctor said. I found out later that my best friend, Mary, lost over a half-stone during this time. The only one who was blissfully calm and blooming in every way was myself. I had my special time every day, thanking God for my continued good health, journalling away happily, 'floating on the sea of God's love' as it were.

Finally my hour came. The baby was very big, was the wrong way round and the cord was around her neck. I had to have a Caesarian section but was safely delivered of a beautiful 8lb 1oz baby girl. Everyone breathed a sigh of relief, especially the doctors.

In spite of everyone's misgivings, God had laid his hand on me in that church that morning and had truly healed me. I was given a second chance at motherhood that I hadn't even asked for. Sometimes, something is so obvious that people refuse to see it. For me it was a miracle and for those who also believed and had prayed with me and for me, it was too.

But for the doctors, it was a different story. Our lovely baby daughter, Sinead, was only six weeks old when I got a call from the hospital. I was informed they wanted me in for another chemotherapy session. I had no idea this was on the cards and had never been warned that it might be, especially so soon after the birth. To me, I was finished with all that. To them, it was obviously a different story. I baulked at first, refusing to go. Who would mind the baby? They rang back with a plan. I could be accommodated in Holles Street, the baby would be minded in the nursery and a doctor would come from Vincent's Hospital every day to administer the drugs. They really thought this was in my best interest. I knew I was healed and didn't need this. The doctors didn't believe any such thing, so I decided, more to placate them than any other reason, to go.

And so I had my last five days of chemotherapy that had begun in 1977, nearly four years previously.

CHAPTER NINE

Pregnant again

That was the last chemo session I ever had and I eventually got home to get on with the wonderful if sometimes terrifying challenge of rearing our little daughter. Both of us were clueless where little babies were concerned. Neither of us had ever changed a nappy in our lives and the night feeds left us drained and exhausted. I think the baby thrived on love rather than proper management for the first three months.

In fact, the weeks flew by. Sinead settled at night and there was light and sleep at the end of the tunnel for us again. We began to really enjoy and take delight in our little baby. I had to attend the hospital very regularly for blood tests but my blood was staying within the normal range and life was very good.

It was so good in fact that six months later I found I was pregnant again! The doctors at this stage must have thought I was a bit of a 'spacer'. 'Is this girl a glutton for punishment? Is she really that stupid that she is still not aware of the risk she is taking with her own health?' Was I not grateful for what I had? What was I thinking of?

The problem was, they were afraid. I wasn't. To me, not only had I been healed but now we were to be doubly blessed. I had a trouble-free pregnancy again and in September 82 we had a beautiful baby boy whom we named Rory. While the doctors were climbing the walls, I had never felt so content in my life. I had to have a C section again as he was in the same position as Sinead had been, but I recovered very quickly and am very proud to say I successfully nursed him for nine months. We now had two lovely children, I was well and back at work.

It's amazing how we can be so thankful and stay so close to God in time of need. It is equally amazing, appalling even, how we can slip so easily back into our old habits. Look at the leper who came back to say thanks. For how long did the excitement last? He owed his new healthy life to his encounter with Jesus. For how long was he thankful? We're not told. Did he go round telling all he met of his good fortune? How long did it take for him to slip back into family life and work? Does our own nature as human beings get in the way of progress towards a deeper relationship with God? It is so easy to be fooled into thinking that the worst is over. I can manage on my own now. By some grace or luck or intuition I had managed to stay faithful to my quiet time, my special time, even if I could only grab a few minutes.

Teresa of Avila once said, 'Settle yourself in solitude and you will come upon him in yourself.' I was drawn into giving thanks again for all the little things. I got back to living just for now, living in the immediate as it were. We were a very normal couple with all the ups and downs of married life, dealing with bills, fractious babies and all the ordinary things that life throws at you. You could have a good week and then an anxious one, etc.

One thing I found very difficult around this time, hurtful even, was how quickly people forgot about the birth of our first baby. The baby was delivered on the ninth of November and every year as that date came round again all the nightmare of the birth would loom again. I was wishing I could go to bed on the 8th and wake up on the 10th. Nobody seemed to remember anymore except myself and Sean. Mind you we didn't remind anyone! Sometimes it's up to yourself to cry for help. Healing of those memories wasn't to come for another thirty years.

God was still in the picture though, there in the background. I was still involved in Renewal and found great blessing and support in our weekly small prayer group. In attending a prayer group you are asked to prepare for it so that you will come with something to share. This really helped to keep me focused, especially as the leadership of the meeting was rotated at the time.

By reading all the wonderful things Jesus said and did, following his guidelines as a lifestyle seemed a good way to go, but for me it certainly hadn't been easy. Doing your utmost to do things the Christian way has to be one of the most difficult roads you could take, especially with an independent nature like mine. To this day, I'm still inclined to row in, sort it out, go headlong towards what I think is the solution. I've got a little better at stopping short and listening and consulting, but probably only a little. I'm still Mary the fixer, and Jesus has a long way to go and a lot to teach me yet. It's difficult to 'let go and let God'.

I should know by now that there is a right time to make a decision or to change a plan, but I've never been good at waiting. St Paul speaks of 'patient endurance'. Some one else said 'All thing come to him who waits.' It's getting good at the waiting that's the problem!

If you think about it, Jesus never promised it would be easy. He just said he would be there. One thing that was very much with me during those years, was my experience in Kilnamanagh church. To me, there was huge healing in the reception of the Eucharist, as well as grace and strength for the moment and I had remained faithful, attending Mass as often as I could. It was totally irrelevant to me what sort of priest was on the altar, young, old, boring, it was of no consequence. No priest would ever change what I had experienced that morning. I'll remember and be thankful until the day I die. I also have the courage to tell people what happened when I'm asked why I still go to Mass after all the scandals etc. It doesn't bother me what they think. I tell my story and they can make what they like of it.

I got a confirmation of the importance of the Eucharist on a recent trip to Medugorje. One of the visionaries gave us this account of a conversation she had with Our Lady one morning. She told Our Lady that she had seen her and she was beautiful but she would love if she brought Jesus with her sometime so she could see him too. Shortly after that she was in bed with a cold and Mary appeared to her as usual. 'Would you really like to meet Jesus?' asked Mary. 'Oh yes,' said Maria. 'Then tomorrow morning get up, put on your best dress and comb your hair. Jesus is coming at 10 0'clock.' Maria did what she was told and sure enough at 10 o'clock there was a knock at the door. Maria rushed to open it all excited, and there stood the priest with the Eucharist! If we could only remind ourselves of the magnitude of what was happening, wouldn't we too prepare well before approaching the altar?

Daily life as we all know can be fraught with anxieties, illness, frustration and disappointment and for me it's certainly no different. You're praying like mad and very faithfully, coming before God sincerely asking for help or guidance. I got a reading, I think it's from St James, that I mulled over for a long time: 'You ask and do not receive because you ask wrongly.' I found this a very difficult passage. How do you ask rightly? Don't we all ask for what we think we need? How do we know?

I got another reading another time from St Paul which helped a tiny bit: 'We cannot boast of having wisdom –

only God is wisdom, but we can tap into it, which empowers us and gives us life.'

So I suppose all we can do is 'tap' away and hope we get the wisdom we need.

My tapping didn't get me very far, or else I had a false notion of what wisdom was or even what was good for me. In 1987, I found I was pregnant again and was delighted. Since our first child was still-born and I needed C sections on the other babies, I decided I would really, really love a natural birth this time. Oh, I believed in God's plan and his wisdom and thanked him daily for my on-going good health. 'Ask and it shall be given', ignore the bit about asking for the right thing, or the wisdom bit, put your faith in God and all would be well.

And it was – in the end – but not before I had learned the most important lesson in my life to date.

CHAPTER TEN

Birth of Barry

My due date came and went, but was I worried? Not me! After all, I had been praying constantly, believing absolutely and even fasting regularly. I had covered every angle. I fully trusted that God noted everything and would take it from here.

Two weeks later, my waters finally broke and in I went. I had asked for the experience of a natural birth and was really looking forward to it. And do you know what? It was dreadful! The baby was huge, over 10 lbs weight and the labour was very long. As I lay there pouring with sweat and exhausted, it was as if I got an image of Jesus leaning up against the wall of the delivery room, smiling and saying, 'You did ask, didn't you? And I answered, didn't I?'

I had learned a very important lesson that morning. What you want and think you need are not necessarily in your best interests! There I was back following my own agenda again instead of leaving all in the capable hands of the Almighty. I was finally delivered of a bouncing baby boy, whom we named Barry. Maybe God granted my prayer knowing I would learn something very important. He was right!

Barry was a lovely strong, healthy baby and I made a good recovery. The only problem was, he was very slow to settle. Both of the others had settled and slept through the night by three months. Not our Barry! In fact, he never slept through the night until he was three years old. Long after we had returned to work, we were both still exhausted and drained with this baby who would not sleep, except in short bouts, was awake again at the slightest sound and wanted to be entertained when everyone else wanted to sleep. He was coming on in leaps and bounds while we were fading out fast!

I suppose, if any of us knew what was ahead, we would turn back quickly and avoid it, wouldn't we? I was still trying to have my special time, 'trying' being the operative word! Most of the time, I drifted off to sleep. Both of us needed our sleep, so how we ended up with a baby who didn't, remains one of life's mysteries. Often during those three years, we were a bit fractious ourselves, having tiffs and words over nothing. We were constantly exhausted. Not knowing how long this was going to go on for was the worst part. Finally, when he was three years old, I put him down as usual about 9 pm expecting him to be awake with enough slept by 4 or 5 am. I woke myself at 7.30 am realising there hadn't been as much as a bleep from his room. I was nearly afraid to go in and check and did actually, fleetingly think the worst. But there he was playing away with his toys. This was a first, as he always cried and cried looking for company. From that day on, he slept through the night, though he continued to be a very light sleeper for years. Because we were now getting a proper night's sleep, the tension eased and everyone was in better humour.

Having my special time now, I could actually manage to stay awake. I was very aware of my frailty and vulnerability as a human being. I was back in the 'immediate', thankful for small things, taking each day as it came. I was back dipping into scripture again. Of course I was looking for 'nice' readings and sometimes I was getting ones I didn't like. The one about patient endurance came up regularly. Another, (when Joseph was sold as a slave), 'until what he had said came to pass, the Lord tested him'. I began 'selective' reading. If I got a reading that irritated me, I tried again. I wanted something beautiful, poetic, consoling – not what I was getting – readings like 'You have not yet reached the point of shedding your blood.' I had had enough of that for the moment, though I had a sneaking suspicion that there was something else in store in the future.

In the meantime, I got on with life. What is life anyway only a pilgrimage along a road that can be very rocky, full of fear and even danger? Sometimes you have companions to lean on, sometimes not. I think it was around this time that I ditched formal prayer altogether, and instead felt free to talk to Jesus as a friend. I could tell him in no uncertain terms how I felt or how fed up I was. He became more of a companion, a soul mate in whom I could confide, shout at, crawl back to or whatever. I think I spent half my time spitting and fighting with him, and the other half crawling back apologising. But best friends are not put off by little tiffs and we were still talking, still very much in touch. Mind you, it was me doing most of the talking and him getting a word in every now and then!

I read somewhere that creation is a on-going thing. We are constantly in a state of change. God is constantly trying to melt me, mould me, change me into what he always planned me to be. So why do I still insist on resisting him? It seems that with every little pearl of wisdom I pick up along the way and treasure, I take ten steps back into the 'old' Mary, who still after all this time, wanders back into 'taking control'.

I have got much better at being silent, at listening. I have to pray every day to stop 'doing', racing ahead, my eye on my own agenda. God has a hard road ahead and I have a long way to go before I allow him to take control over my life. I lapse every day. He hauls me back and on it goes. If I was him, I would have given up on me years ago!

I'm reminded of Peter, whom Jesus chose to lead his church – a weak man who was very afraid and then hugely repentant – what did Jesus see in him? He obviously could see qualities in Peter not apparent to anyone else. I like to think that Jesus sees qualities in all of us that could be put to good use for the good of others, to help each other, if only we would take that leap of faith and say 'Yes, use me if you like.'

I used to have this terrible fear, or caution that if I ever asked him to use me, he might ask me to leave my house and comfort and move to Africa or something. Now I think a little differently. It's more about trust, handing over, getting rid of that anxiety, that stumbling block that can inhibit your growth, your on-going creation. Let's face it, very few of us will ever be asked to uproot ourselves to the extent that Abraham had to. It's more to do with constantly changing, hopefully moving closer to Jesus, who can and will direct you in the tiniest detail of your life. The trick is, to *let* him, to listen, to be silent. You will get a thought, an idea, or a strength to get through the day. I pray every day that I will stop talking, stop giving out, learn to be very quiet. I know that it's only in the silence that I will find peace. I try to be open to what he might be saying. I pray for the grace to take heed. I'm so very glad I had learned this much along the way. I was going to need every drop of wisdom, every ounce of courage, for the next huge hurdle in my life, which was temporarily to affect our marriage and leave us all deeply scarred.

Jesus wasn't finished with me yet. All along, he had been preparing me for the next shock which began to emerge in late 01 and through 02. A reading I got for this time was 'turn to me and be safe'. And another that kept appearing, 'I can do all things in him who strengthens me'

I knew something was wrong. It took two years to have it diagnosed. I had reached another mountain I had to climb, but this time there was no map to show me the way down the other side.

CHAPTER ELEVEN

A brain tumour

All through the year 02, I was noticing subtle changes in my body and mind. Sometimes I would lean down to get something out of the bottom of the fridge and just fall, just keel over without any apparent reason. Other times, people would come up to me, at school or at the shops, and ask me if I was alright. To me, I was fine – I didn't know what they were talking about. I felt very well, though for some reason I was walking more slowly and carefully, looking out for something I might trip over. Sometimes as well, during the night I would wake up with a very bad headache. No pill or medication or even a cup of tea helped at all. The only way to get relief was to sit upright for about an hour.

I was driving, as I had been for years without incident or accident. All of a sudden, Sean would start getting very tense, telling me I was on the wrong side of the road. Of course I wasn't. What a stupid thing to accuse me of! On it went and anytime Sean was in the car with me, the tension mounted. I don't think he ever trusted a female driver, but this was ridiculous. Now we were having regular shouting matches with him sometimes grabbing the wheel and I totally humiliated. As I saw it, I was driving normally. He disagreed, to put it mildly. As the tension mounted, the rows continued. Sometimes days passed without a word spoken between us. At this stage, I began to have 'little accidents' on the road, where I would 'skim' another car, not realising how close I was to it. Now there were rows with other drivers as well as rows at home. My spatial judgement was getting very bad. I had my first accident, slamming into the back bumper of a car going into the shopping centre, again having no idea I was so close.

Things at home were going from bad to worse. I decided to have my eyes checked. The optician spotted something and referred me on to an eye specialist to check it out. I went and was told there was nothing wrong with my sight. I discovered afterwards that due to huge pressure from one side of my brain, I had actually lost the sight in my left eye at this stage. How he missed that is a mystery.

Around this time as well, I woke during the night and thought I heard the TV still on downstairs. I went down to check it out and if I did, I lost my footing and balance and fell down the stairs. Thinking I was just a bit bruised, I got myself back up to bed. No-one had actually heard me! The next morning I had to announce that I had another problem, my right foot was the size of a large balloon. Sean drove me to A and E. The atmosphere between us was awful, a pregnant silence. I knew he was getting fed up with the whole scenario. I now had to take eight weeks off work as I had three broken toes and was on crutches.

Life continued and things eased a bit between us. I couldn't drive, which I think helped matters. The weeks passed, my foot healed and back I went to work. I wasn't comfortable driving anymore. I had lost all my confidence. Sean would drop me to school and I would get the bus home. Thankfully there were no more accidents, though we were still having little 'tiffs'.

Apparently, when eating my dinner, especially when putting something on my plate, I often missed the plate completely, with the food ending up on the table or the floor. I was getting messy and incompetent, both characteristically not like me at all. I went to the doctor, I think with a chest infection or something, and spilled out my whole story of how distressing life was becoming. He didn't say a whole lot but obviously suspected something and referred me on to a neurologist in the Mater Hospital. That's when the fun started. The first available appointment with him was nine months away! I suspected myself, and so did everyone else, that this was too long of a wait. The doctor gave me another letter stressing the urgency of a check-up, all to no avail. It made no difference at all. In the meantime, I continued to fall and to bang into doors and presses.

One day, I had to drive. It was during the time of all the curricular changes in education, and we were having lots of in-service training days. I had managed up to this to either get a lift or take a bus, but decided to chance this one as it was very close to home and there was no direct bus route. It was to be held in Moran's Hotel. I could take the back road through Ballymount. I would be there in ten minutes. Off I went and successfully got to the venue and the day went well. It was when I came out that things began to go horribly wrong. I couldn't for the life of me find the car. I walked up and down the car-park with no success. I got totally confused and very upset. All the others had gone and I was still rambling around. Eventually I found the car, but then I came out the wrong exit and was heading north instead of back towards Tallaght. All I can remember of that awful day is how confused and upset I was, thinking how everyone at home would raise their eyes to heaven and wonder how I could possibly be so stupid.

I was really very frightened and the idea began to dawn on me that I might have Alzheimers. Everything I had ever read about the condition came back into my head. I bawled, I prayed, I cried again. I eventually got home in an awful state. Sean wasn't laughing or giving out. I could see he was quite worried himself. He had a cousin who worked in administration in the Mater Hospital who was on the look-out for a cancellation but to no avail. There seemed nothing for it but to wait.

Then one night, we went out for a meal, Sean, myself and his mother. On leaving the restaurant, I completely missed the edge of the path and fell out onto the road and into the traffic. We all got a bad fright. We left Sean's mother home and it's then Sean decided enough was enough. We packed a bag, made sure everyone at home was okay and headed for the hospital. As far as I can remember, they couldn't find any record of my appointment! But Sean wasn't leaving without someone seeing me. I was put on a trolley to wait – nothing new there! A doctor came along after a while to do a few preliminary tests. I think they knew immediately what was wrong but said nothing. One of the tests was to get me to walk a straight line, which of course I couldn't. I knew I wasn't drunk and made sure I told them so. They asked me to subtract seven from 100. I couldn't do that either, at least not for about five minutes or so. I felt confused and humiliated all over again. Eventually, after some hours, they admitted me for an MRI scan which they said would be done the following morning. In a way I was relieved. Surely something would show up and hopefully it wouldn't be Alzheimers.

Sean went home to the family to get a few hours rest and I was put to bed. All I remember of that room is, the walls were grey, my mood was equally grey, and looking out the window, all I could see was the grey walls of Mountjoy Prison. All this time, I had been praying, talking to Jesus, asking for wisdom to understand what was going on, and now at least I was going to get an answer. I wasn't so sure I wanted to know. Was I ready for what was to happen next? Could I really trust and hand it over? I tried to think of positive things rather than negative. Maybe the news wouldn't be that bad.

Later that day a very junior doctor came into me and one look at her face said it all. It wasn't good news.' Is your husband here?' she enquired. When I said he was at work but was on the alert waiting for news, she went out and must have sent for Sean. She came back with the news that I had a very large brain tumour. It was taking up a huge amount of space on the right side of my brain. She explained that the pressure was great, hence the headaches and loss of my sight in my left eye. She thought it was probably benign but they wouldn't be sure until after an operation. There was nothing for it. I had to have surgery. It would continue to grow and had to come out. It was in a good position and the chances were good that they would get it all out.

To say I was stunned would be an understatement. I had absolutely nothing to say to the girl – no questions – nothing. In one sense, everything was now clear, the headaches, loss of balance, confusion, all was now revealed. I tried to cheer myself up thinking at least it's not Alzheimers, the thing I think I most dreaded.

Sean arrived looking ashen. Nobody can look quite as pale or shaken as a redhead! We just sat there holding hands and saying very little.

I remember looking at him who had stayed so faithful through all the years of my illnesses. I knew he was going to 'rally' again and thanked God for his support. I knew I wasn't going to be on my own, no matter what the consequences were. The next night in the hospital was a long one. I was on my own. There was no disturbance, good or bad. I had all night to come to terms with the news, to think things through. The most frightening part, I suppose, was I was heading into unknown territory, putting my whole life into the hands of this surgeon, not knowing if I would ever wake up or if I did, what state I would be in.

One half of me was very frightened, the other half re-minding myself of what I had come through in the past. The only thing for it was to trust again. To leave every-thing in the hands of God. I spent the whole night trying to do this but I'm afraid my humanity and frailty got in the way. I remembered the quote, 'Nothing is impossible with God.' I prayed for the help I knew I would need to get through this.

All my fears came to the fore. I found I was tortured with worry, not so much for myself but for my family. How would Sean cope? Would he remarry? I thought of each of the children, all very different in personality. How would my death affect them? Would they stay close, share their worries, support each other? There I was again – the mother hen! A mother probably never fully lets go of her brood.

I must have finally drifted off to sleep because the next thing I knew someone was at the door with a breakfast tray. Of course, I missed half of the food that was on that tray and some probably ended up on the floor, but at least now I knew why. It wasn't me who had become awkward and clumsy, it was that I couldn't see properly. Knowing that in itself made me more relaxed and peaceful.

When the nurses came in to make the bed and realised my dilemma, they were very helpful and turned up at other mealtimes to help or guide my hand.

The news came that I was to be transferred for priority surgery to Beaumont Hospital the following Wednesday. This, I think was either Monday or Tuesday so I didn't have long to wait. I began to unwind in the room, to relax and found Jesus putting positive thoughts in my head.

'Who said this was the end?' I also remembered that lovely story about the footsteps in the sand. If you can only see one set of footsteps it's because Jesus is carrying you. All indications led back to that promise: 'Be not afraid, I go before you always.' I was reminded of all the things I had to be thankful for and I did thank God. We had three beautiful children, all healthy. If my life on earth was nearly over, he was hardly going to abandon them now, was he?

I had been very blessed up to this. I had a good sense that all would be well. I was beginning to feel quite peaceful.

That is, until a nurse arrived in with a pill. I wasn't on any medication and enquired what it was for. 'Oh, that's in case you develop epileptic fits after the surgery,' she announced breezily. Well, I needn't tell you, all my peace and tranquility went out the window and I was back to Square 1. If anxiety and worry were to be put on a scale of 1-10 at that point in time, I was easily as far as an 8 or 9.

No-one should ever be left on their own in a room in a hospital if at all possible. You have all day to dwell on this operation. I was trying to prevent myself from dwelling on possible side effects. Epilepsy, paralysis, blindness, deafness – I didn't want to know. I stopped asking questions. I ploughed on with my special prayer time, I journalled, I wrote poems, all in writing that, looking at it now, was practically illegible because of my blindness.

The time came for my transfer to Beaumont and the only prayer I said was, 'Jesus, hold my hand, walk the road with me, stay close.'

CHAPTER TWELVE

Operation for tumour

Arriving in Beaumont Hospital, I was admitted into a six-bed ward. I was made very welcome by the other patients and the nursing staff were looking after my every comfort. On chatting to everyone else, I discovered we were all due for imminent surgery for the removal of all sorts of tumours from brain to base of the spine. When it came to the first meal-time there, everyone else could eat normally except me. I had to ask a nurse for help as I couldn't see half the food on the plate let alone cut it up and guide it safely to my mouth. She went off and returned with something that looked like a bib but I had to wear it to save my night-gown or else eat nothing. I found it so difficult to accept this graciously. I was acutely embarrassed and wished I was in a room on my own so no-one would notice. After a day or two, I realised no-one noticed at all, or if they did they were very helpful. It was myself and my stupid pride and independence that were to blame.

Looking around and listening to everyone else's stories, we all had enough fears and anxieties of our own to pre-occupy us, and what was happening to someone else was only secondary. The day was very long, as I couldn't read at all now. I tried journalling but most of what I wrote was totally illegible. I had my visitors, my family, my faithful friends (guardian angels) and when they left in the evening I talked a lot to God, bringing all my fears and humiliation, though I don't think I actually handed them over! But at least I was trying.

Then came D-Day. I was for the knife, saw or whatever the next day. In fact, the whole ward were to be brought down the next day, all at different times. My time was 8.15 am. When we all got the news, there was a silence for a while as we drank it in, and possibly a little relief as well. The sooner it was done, the sooner it would be over. We were all to fast from midnight. They offered us a 'big tea' the evening before if we wished. I, for one, didn't touch a thing. To me, it sounded too much like a last meal before execution or something.

I don't know if any of us slept well that night, I know I didn't. All my thoughts were full of anxiety, full of fear, all the 'what ifs' came back to haunt me – blindness, paralysis, epilepsy, all reared their ugly heads. I remembered again Jesus in the garden of Gethsemane. He knew what was ahead and according to the gospels, he sweated blood he was so terrified. He asked God to take this cross away from him. He realised this was what was ahead of him. He was able to say, 'Not my will but thine be done.' It was alright to be afraid. Jesus understood.

At some stage during that long night, being reminded again of all the times I had been blessed in the past, I prayed for the grace to get through this and the strength to accept whatever might lie ahead. Eventually, I must have fallen asleep because I had to be woken up the next morning to be gowned, etc. I hadn't got a minute to myself and before I knew it, I was on the trolley and on my way. For some reason, I remembered a reading I had had a good while back, when I could still read – ' On waking, I shall be content in your presence.' With these words in my head, I knew that Jesus had never left and was now walking beside me holding my hand. I was actually very peaceful. I felt protected and loved and safe. I sensed Sean and all my family around me and drew strength from it. I had a lovely feeling of well-being as I was wheeled into the theatre and introduced to the operating team.

Post-Op

My first vague memory after the operation was being aware of Sean, Sinead, and my sister-in-law, Mary – hearing voices, someone saying 'Thank God.' Then I seemed to be 'out of it' for a long time. All I wanted to do was sleep.

A nurse seemed to be pestering me to wake up, answer questions, open my eyes. All I wanted was to be left alone. The 'pestering' went on and on – Mary, when is your birthday? What is your address? Who is the President of Ireland? Eventually, I had emerged out of the anaesthetic to be aware of the nurse approaching again. To get some peace, I answered all the questions in one go before the nurse even got started! He just smiled and said, 'She's fine', and left.

The operation, I'm told, took about nine hours but they were confident they had removed all of the tumour. That was good news. I spent a few days in a 'high-dependency' ward before being transferred back to an ordinary ward. I was full of tubes, I had a catheter, I had a tube to drain my brain, but I must say I was in no pain as such. I opened one eye first, a little apprehensively and my vision seemed to be fine. Then I tried to open the 'bad' one, to find it was covered with a bandage. Apparently, they had scratched the surface of it during the operation, so I still didn't know whether I had my vision back in that eye. There was more patience needed and I wouldn't actually know for a few days yet. I was back in the same ward, with the same people. We were now all 'post-op'. The ward was very quiet as we recovered. All of the operations had been successful. Everyone had good news, though we were all still a bit too wobbly to appreciate it. I still had to be fed as my eye was still covered. I was cheerfully told by a nurse that the hair on one half of my head had been shaved off and I had 57 staples in my skull. This didn't bother me at all, as I presumed they would have to do some shaving, but why didn't they shave it all off while they were at it? I hadn't yet seen myself, but how freaky was I going to look with half a head of hair? Luckily, I could see the funny side of it. After all, I couldn't expect a brain surgeon to be interested in the cosmetic side of things.

I was reading again with my one good eye, and was having my special time, late at night. I was once more able to thank God for what I had and to leave things in his hands regarding my other eye. I was getting lovely positive, reassuring readings, e.g. 'My body abides in confidence, because you will not abandon my soul'

As I said before, a day in a hospital can seem endless. But I was healing very fast and after five days, the catheter was gone, the drip was gone, the brain drain was removed and they finally took the patch off my eye for good. They had been removing it at regular intervals only to apply more ointment, so up to this I still didn't know if my sight was back. When the bandage came off for good, I must say, I was quite apprehensive about opening that eye. After all, I hadn't been able to see through it for months. I said a quick prayer. It went something like this: 'Lord, it would be wonderful if I could see just a little bit, enough to stop banging into things, enough to read and write a little. I'd be happy with that.' I opened my eye. I thought I could see perfectly. Could I? Everything seemed normal. I got a book and started to read. Lo and behold, I could read perfectly. Everything was so clear. My vision was back! My dinner arrived. I could see it and eat it on my own! What a day this was!

The doctors arrived later on and proclaimed that there

had been no lasting damage to my eye. The tumour was gone, the pressure was off, my sight was back.

I think I spent the rest of that day 'on a high', without any drugs!

I began to reflect a bit, to look back on the last twenty-five years and to wonder what it was all about. I nearly died then. I didn't. Why? Is there a message here? Is there something I'm supposed to learn from all this? If there is, am I listening?

Emerging once again, on the road to recovery, battered and bruised, do I want to hear? 'Follow me,' you said, 'and you shall have rest'. Well, you must have meant eventually! Is there something I'm meant to do? If there is, could you put it on hold for a while? Give me a little break?

I suppose, life is a constant learning experience, full of change, some terrible times, some good. At that moment in time I remember thinking, if there's something I'm being prepared for, something I'm meant to do, I'm not ready yet for any more challenges at this point.

I just felt like diving into a cave for a while, the bliss of total withdrawal from everything, rest, total rest is what I crave. I'm done.

CHAPTER THIRTEEN

Home again

I left Beaumont in high good humour just two weeks after the operation. Because I read so much, the one blessing I had been asking for was that I would retain my eyesight, such a little thing for God, such a huge plus for me. There was nothing better on a wet day than to curl up on your favourite armchair with a good book. One half of me was trying to leave everything in God's hands, the other half hoping against hope that the healing would include my eyesight. God, in his love, indulged me, as not only was my eyesight back to normal but my balance was as well. I was walking freely and properly, I was smiling broadly and was more than ready to get on with everyday things.

I was warned to take things very easy, and to have someone with me all the time for a while. Sean took leave from work, my sister Pauline arrived from England, my elderly mother arrived, my daughter Sinead rang or called in every day. My brother was calling and the neighbours were wonderful. As my strength increased, I felt more and more that I could cope better and actually get more rest on my own. I was beginning to feel 'swamped'. I knew they were all concerned but after a week or two, I very politely 'shooed' them all away and sent Sean back to work. I was worn out entertaining visitors and talking to people, even though I really appreciated the love and the care.

I now had room to breathe, to put a bit of structure on my day. I knew if I didn't get organised, the day would be very long and I would be very bored. I organised little things to do, to pass a half-hour or so, as I wasn't up to much as yet. I got back to journalling and to my special time mostly being still and just listening. Believe me, I find this an onward challenge, just 'to be'.

Maybe the habit of organising a class full of children for so long made it harder. I liked school, I liked a challenge and here I was sitting at home all day with none. I listened to music, I sang to myself, I read, but I still found the day dragged. I was actually feeling quite depressed as if the walls were closing in around me.

One day, I got an idea. 'Have a bath by yourself.' Now this may seem very strange to you, but you see, since my balance went, I always had Sean around either getting me in and out of the bath or staying in the vicinity, in case I fell. Since I came home, I still had him waiting outside the door, just in case. This was a real challenge and I sensed Jesus asking me to trust him for this little thing – Sean wasn't here now, he was at work. How did this idea get into my head? Was I foolish to try this? After all, God gave me common sense, didn't he expect me to use it? The idea persisted and finally I decided to try it. All doubts and memories came flooding back. You'll slip and fall, you'll never get out by yourself. There's no-one in the house to help. But I still sensed that I should do it and up I went. I said to myself, don't worry about getting out, just fill it up, put in lovely bath oil, get your fluffiest towel and get in. I did. I had the most wonderful time in that bath, just soaking up the heat, relaxing in the bubbles. I found I had no fear at all about getting out or falling. My confidence was coming back. With a quick prayer asking Jesus to hold my hand, out I jumped. No problem at all! What I did then I still laugh about today. I jumped back in again, then out, then in, then out again, just delighting in the notion that my balance seemed to be back. Another small mountain climbed and conquered!

I got dressed, singing at the top of my voice, when another idea came into my head – 'Walk down the stairs.' Up to this, I had either come down on my bum or clinging very tightly to the banisters. I could still see the stairs rising to meet me as I fell that time and broke my toes. I had never really regained my confidence and had never, ever taken the chance of walking freely down the stairs. The very thought of it terrified me. I had words with Jesus. Isn't one challenge enough for one day? I rose to the challenge of the bath didn't I? Couldn't I leave this one until tomorrow? I promise, I'll try it then.

All the time I was sick, I thanked him for good days. I told him I trusted him, but did I really? Was it all just words? That Charismatic song that I loved and sang so often came into my head – 'Though the mountains crumble and disappear, I will be with you, you need have no fear.'

I suppose years ago, as children, we all learnt off all those catechism answers without a clue as to what they were about. I certainly didn't dwell too deeply on any of it. To me, it was a case of, 'Learn it, recite it, keep the teacher happy.' Had I moved on at all from there? Did I ever really listen to and believe in the words of Jesus or was I still just singing a nice song?

I sang it again, very slowly this time, told Jesus I trusted as much as I was able, and headed for the top of the stairs. If I didn't really believe or trust all my prayers, all my conversations with him would mean nothing, just lip service, just shallow prayers. Is that what I believed? I knew it wasn't. I remembered again that extraordinary experience in the church with the Eucharist, and I knew deep down that I did believe. So now I was going to trust. I put my foot on the first step, then the next, then the next. I was still standing. The stairs hadn't moved. It must have taken me about ten minutes to get the whole way down and it definitely was the longest ten minutes of my life, but I got there safe and sound. I hadn't fallen. I had not got dizzy but probably lost a few pounds weight with the strain of it all. I think I learned that day that even in a minute of prayer or during a quiet time, I do most of the talking with very little listening to anything God might want to say. I had a long way to go to reach that point of stillness where I listened and could learn something.

In spite of myself, I was learning a lot about myself. I go back to the point I made earlier about creation being an on-going thing. We are constantly learning, changing, being moulded into maybe what God always planned us to be and do. I can't move on if I don't accept change and I won't grow if I'm not prepared to listen. I won't hear if I don't find time to be still.

That's the hardest challenge for me. To leave that 'list' of things to do, problems to be tackled, people to ring, bills to pay etc. To be able to leave all that aside for a few minutes, withdraw from the 'frenzy' of life and just 'be', just 'float on the sea of God's love'.

I found that if I practised this every day, the important things ended up getting done anyway. Things got slowly better for me. I organised my day, grew in confidence, got back to a bit of gardening, was allowed to drive again and finally after four months, rather than the six they predicted, I got back to work. Lots of people were still keeping in touch, I was surrounded by love and encouragement. I was back to normal.

Looking back on my journals of that time, there were a few scary times that still persist to this day. At first my speech would slur at the drop of a hat, which was embarrassing if I was talking to a neighbour. I also got blinding headaches every now and then, but they finally stopped and my head settled down. Sometimes, as well, my memory slips – e.g. I might be looking for the bread knife or something. I would have a picture of the knife in my head but I can't for the life of me remember what it's called. That is still happening today, but I don't worry about it. For the most part, life is good. I can work, read, drive, do everything necessary to get on with the day.

We had a lovely holiday in Croatia that summer and yes, life was good again, for now.

CHAPTER FOURTEEN

A hysterectomy and a wonderful healing

It was now 2003. I was back at work fulltime and life had returned to normal again. My confidence when driving was still very dodgy. I must have had the only car in Ireland where strings of aspirations were uttered before I even turned the key! I prayed at every junction, I spent most of every journey praying, and was very thankful every time I arrived safely home. Regaining your confidence is a slow and agonising journey, peppered with memories of the past, skimming cars, losing my way, etc. I figured I needed every grace and blessing I could get. But, thank God, I never had another accident. I still lose my way, but I never had a great sense of direction anyway. Sean is very nervous if he is in the car with me driving, but I don't think that's to do with tumours. As I said before, I doubt if he ever fully trusted women drivers in the first place!

Life went on, as it tends to do, fairly smoothly. I was beginning to develop 'womens' problems' – irregular periods, very swollen tummy, a lot of discomfort but I was now fifty-one years old and presumed it was the beginning of menopause. I must say I ignored a lot of the symptoms for a while and wasn't particularly worried.

My blood pressure has been unstable for years and I went to my doctor for my regular check-up. Being a good doctor, he gave me a thorough examination and asked loads of questions. I left the surgery with a letter of referral to a gynecologist, 'Just to check things out' as he said. I had the usual scan, and the news was 'You have a womb full of fibroids as well as adhesions probably there for years. You're a bit of a mess really. You need a hysterectomy.'

You can imagine my reaction – more surgery, more hospitalisation, more time out of school. I was just back to normal life. 'Will they not go away by themselves?' I asked in all innocence. What a daft question! I was for the 'chop' again and that was all there was to it. How will this news go down with Sean, with the family, with school, with friends? All the time of course, it was myself who had to come to terms with it.

After two false starts and two cancelled appointments in Tallaght Hospital, I finally got a bed in the Coombe Maternity Hospital, where the doctor assured me, the night before surgery, I would be a new woman afterwards. 'You won't know yourself,' he said.

I was getting quite *blasé* about hospitals at this stage and if I had had a third hand I could have done the blood tests myself. I got a lovely reading the night before the operation:

> When I thought my foot slips,
> your steadfast love, O Lord, held me up.
> When the cares of my heart are many
> your consolations cheer my soul.
> The Lord has become my stronghold
> and my God the rock of my refuge.

That's it! All will be well. I went to sleep and slept like a log.

Everything did go very well. The doctor called in to say I'd given him a bit of work to do. It took them a while to remove all the fibroids before they even got started on the adhesions. He kept assuring me that I would be a new woman, though I don't think I've yet got to that stage. However, my recovery went well, though there were some very bad, very low days. I developed a urinary tract infection, which was to recur again several times in the months that followed. While still in the hospital, I was very depressed. The length of the day and the fact that I was so immobile didn't help. All of my memories of previous hospitalisation and things that went wrong loomed in front of me and the tears flowed freely. Why did all these things happen to me? Why did other people seem to escape so freely and seem to have a grand healthy life free from illness?

This was more or less the state the hospital chaplain found me in when she called to see me. I ended up pouring out my whole history, whether she had time to hear it or not. When she heard about the loss of our first baby, she suggested I needed a bit of closure. She asked if I would like to visit the little mortuary in the hospital where they had it specially set up for neo-natal and still-born babies. She knew we had never had a funeral or even got to say goodbye. She went away and asked me to think about it. She would come back the next morning – no pressure, but she would arrange it if I wished.

When she came back the next day, I had decided I would go with her, if only to pass an hour, to break the monotony of the day. Little did I know what was in store for me.

Patricia went off and got a wheelchair and permission to take me over to the oratory. We had to go out of the main building and across to the little chapel. She had actually done out a leaflet with our baby's name on it. This was going to be the first and only little service for Marie-Claire. One part of me was curious, another part, apprehensive. When we got there, she opened the door and in we went. I found I was shocked to the core. There in the centre, was an empty Moses basket, all done up in white. The place was cold and to me was filled with a terrible sense of loss and sorrow and grief. I wasn't sure I wanted to go ahead with it. This was like the funeral we never had and I found my grief was as raw as ever.

She began the little prayers anyway and I cried and cried and cried. There were discreet boxes of tissues left around that definitely must have been replenished very often if I was anything to go by. She said we could stay as long as I wanted to. I looked at the empty crib. I cried again. There was a silence there, a coldness of death, of finality, though in a strange way, there was also a sense of peace. I had accepted and known for years that my baby was a very real little soul who was now perfectly at peace in heaven. I had long chat with her, regretting as her mam that I hadn't got to know her, to rear her. I told her about her dad, her sister and brothers, and how I still really missed her, especially on the anniversary of her birth.

It was a good long time before I was ready to leave. I did get a sense of relief if not peace, when the tears finally abated. We headed back over to the main hospital and what did God do to 'lighten the load' as it were? The wheel came off the wheelchair! There I was, in a flimsy dressing gown, out in the cold in the month of March with my mode of transport gone. When I heard the language out of the hospital chaplain, I suddenly could see the funny side of it and started to laugh. I had to hobble back into the mortuary while she went off to find a porter and another wheelchair. Thus was the bubble of that awful solemn hour burst and a little bit of fun and laughter crept in. We eventually made it back to the main hospital, very cold but intact (mentally and physically) and Patricia treated me to a muffin and a coffee in the coffee shop.

When I finally got back to the ward, I was in better humour. I had got a little bit of closure and felt a bit freer to move on. I think I was carrying the burden of that grief for years and it had never been dealt with or resolved. I could feel a new peace, a new lift, a new healing.

God had intervened again. He knows me inside-out. I'm glad my bed was not available in Tallaght and that I ended up in the Coombe instead. I badly needed that closure. I had thought I had moved on, as the years went by. I wasn't upset anymore on her birthday. Obviously, God knew it hadn't been dealt with properly and moved in when the time was right. Now it was brought to the fore, to be presented to God for healing. I found it extremely painful emotionally, but in the end worthwhile. I was able to move on more freely now. Thank God for his plan. We sometimes don't like his methods or his 'pruning', but I could see what he was up to. It needed to be dealt with and I'm glad it was. Definitely, his ways are not our ways. Sometimes you can feel like 'a lone bird on a roof-top', but you're not on your own – he's there.

CHAPTER FIFTEEN

Another brush with cancer

Home again, a bit battered and bruised but still standing, after a fashion. For the next few months I was plagued with urinary tract infections, which wore me down a bit. I certainly hadn't reached the 'you won't know yourself' bit or anywhere near it. Because I was again housebound for the most part and wasn't allowed to drive, I got very fed up. I had my quiet time but the trouble was, the whole day was too quiet. The 'doer' in me was dying to get going but I wasn't up to much physically. My body just wouldn't respond. I kept my eye on my check-up date, mentally crossing off the days. All would be much better when I was out and about again. I just had to have patience. I had to look at the garden and sometimes force myself not to dig, pull weeds, lift or mow the grass.

The great day dawned eventually, and I must say I was excited. I would get a taxi to the clinic, but wouldn't it be great to come home, pick up the car and go for a drive. Off I went in high spirits to meet with the doctor. 'Can I drive again?' I asked. 'Certainly' came the reply. 'Can I go back to work?' 'I don't see why not.' 'So all is well then,' says I standing up to leave. 'Sit down a second,' says he, studying his notes carefully. And that's when I got the next blow. He explained that every womb removed is routinely sent off after surgery for tests. Mine, unfortunately, showed up positive for cancer.

You know, it's amazing how bad news still took a few minutes to sink in, even after all the times I had had this experience before. You probably never get used to it, or else I'm an eternal optimist. I sat there, he sat there and for a few minutes nothing was said. I know him to be a caring and compassionate man, so it was probably as hard on him as it was on me. I didn't react at all for a few minutes. The ball was back in my court. 'What happens now?' He explained that the womb was now gone and hopefully the cancer was gone with it, but there was no way of telling. He would bring me back for smear tests on a regular basis to see if anything showed up.

Now if I had known I was to get news like that, I would have brought Sean with me. Here I was on my own having to get a taxi home and try and absorb this latest news. I was to be left in 'Limbo' as regards my health. I rang Sean, who wanted to come and pick me up but I said no. I needed time on my own to get used to this new situation. If I needed him later, I would ring. I got into a taxi, and instead of giving him instructions for home, I found myself telling him to drive me to the 'Square Shopping Centre'.

I think one half of me was afraid to go home to an empty house, the other half wanted to scream in pure defiance. Why couldn't I just recover like most other people? I was heartily sick of all these setbacks. Nothing ever seemed to go straightforward for us or not for very long anyhow. When I got to the Shopping Centre, I went into the oratory. That didn't help. How could it? I was screaming in frustration with God and I mean screaming! How could he answer? He couldn't get a word in edgeways! Then I hit the shops, buying things I didn't need at all – not like me. That was my reaction to this latest episode in my life. Eventually, of course , I went home, a bit calmer, a little deflated and I suppose, if the truth were known, a little worried. The whole family were all worried. 'What did he say again? Can you not get further tests to make sure it's gone?' etc. I found with all the questions and the worry, it was as if I was standing apart listening to them all. I discovered that deep down, I didn't think I was quite as worried as they were. Let them worry all they wanted to, about what might happen and it was a 'might', I was going to go for my check-ups, do what I was told and to hell with it! I decided life was too short to worry about all the 'ifs and maybes'. I had enough to be doing keeping up with what is happening now, not next week. I felt fine, I was going back to work and that was that. I actually wasn't a bit anxious at all once I got over the initial shock.

Well, I've been for all my check-ups for the last two years and so far all is well. I think if I didn't know God was there in the background, it would be a different scenario altogether. Imagine carrying the burden of that worry on your own. That doesn't mean that I don't get anxious now and then about an infection or an unexplained ache or pain, it just means that I handle it a little differently. I sit down and ask for guidance, trusting that I'll know if I need to see a doctor or check something out. If I let worry take over my life, it will wear me down, just age me and solve nothing. I don't need that.

CHAPTER SIXTEEN

Early retirement

I'm now 55 years old and took early retirement while my health was very good. There were lots of things I wanted to do that I couldn't possibly fit in while still teaching. One of them was to sit down and write my story.

I was plagued with doubt for about a year beforehand. Hundreds of people have a story worth listening to, most of them much more interesting and definitely more entertaining than mine. I'd never have enough for a book. Who would be bothered publishing it? The idea persisted however and just wouldn't go away. I often gave talks, when asked, at *Life in the Spirit Seminars*, and people would ask, 'Where is your book?' I knew for a while I had to write it down even if it never got published. In doing so, I realised just how much I have learned, about myself, about my own inadequacies, my strengths and weaknesses but mostly I can see so clearly now how close God really was even when I didn't notice. He has nudged me along through all the blisters and pitfalls on this pilgrimage of life.

So what have I learned?

1. I haven't changed basically, I'm still me with all my faults and failings.

2. To me, life is a journey, a pilgrimage. Any pilgrimage I've been on or read about is full of rough stones, blisters and hardship. You'll probably find yourself on the road at times with people you can't get on with, who drive you nuts. You will find at times that you are very tired, you've lost all your energy and enthusiasm for the trek. Maybe your hopes and reasons for doing it in the first place were too high or even the wrong reasons. You expect God to

answer your prayer: 'I'm asking, I'm here, please give.' Maybe you're following your own road, your own dream rather than the plan he has for you. Believe me, from experience, his is a better one!

3. It's not the goal or the end result that's important, but the journey with all its stumbling blocks and disappointments.

4. It's very important to stop now and then, be still, admit you need help. You might even be lost, if only you would admit it.

5. Set aside your own agenda every now and again, stop, ask for guidance. You won't hear or notice anything if you're constantly racing along.

6. I know now that I can't do it all myself. I admit that I need strength, wisdom and guidance at every step. I won't always need courage but it's there for the asking if needed.

7. Wisdom can appear in many guises. Be humble enough to admit that you need it. Be on the look out for it. Learn to notice how near God is.

8. Give everything your best shot and anything you can't handle, just leave it, hand it over and let him who knows best sort it out.

9. God will use you and get through to you through your talents, your strengths and weaknesses. He got through to me through lots of different channels – my love of music and poetry, my tendency to 'scribble' or to journal, my love of reading, even through my imagination. He will work with you where you're at. It is through my hobbies and past-times, through gardening, that he will reach me.

10. He is a very gentle God. He will never be forceful. He will wait patiently until you're ready to acknowledge him.

11. Through practising to be still, I have discovered his presence deep within me rather than through books or study of any kind.

12. I have found a truly wonderful friend and teacher who guides me through every hour.

13. I'm more comfortable now with who I am now. It's okay to be me – hopeless at sport, stones overweight, going grey, developing wrinkles. I don't wish anymore that I had beautiful hair or long legs. I like who I am.

14. I'm better at acknowledging my talents now, such as they are and am willing to use them if called upon. I also acknowledge all my faults and failings but don't regard myself as a failure.

15. I don't just 'believe' anymore, I 'know' that there is a God who is very near.

16. In my human frailty, I slide in and out of trust all the time, but he knows me through and through and he knows I'll always come back.

17. I know I need a special grace to get me through bad days but he understands when I get upset or get bad news.

18. God was always there. I never noticed it until I got sick.

19. I read an awful lot – biographies, historical novels, anything really – and once I came across something Churchill said that I found helpful. 'If you find yourself in hell, keep going.' He too had hopes that things might improve, that there might be light at the end of the tunnel.

20. There is such a huge source of wisdom to tap into, I know that now.

21. In the midst of all the distractions of living, work, dreams, laughter, family, etc, I've learnt that if I withdraw for just a little while each day I actually have more energy and wisdom for whatever the day throws at me. I would probably never have discovered this inner point of stillness if I had never got sick, I'd still be running around chasing my tail. So in that sense, I'm glad things happened as they did.

22. I have experienced the wonderful healing power of God's love and life for me will never be the same again. I

don't try to make sense of it all, it's too vast, too cloudy. I won't see the full picture until I get to heaven and the veil is lifted.

23. It can be a long lonely difficult road at times but wouldn't you rise to any challenge, tackle any problem if you were sure someone was going to be with you every step of the way, holding your hand, picking you up, dealing with all the blisters? As it says in the song: 'Keep your eyes upon Jesus, look full in his wonderful face/so that hour by hour, you may know his power, till at last you have won the great race.'

24. I know that the future will have more obstacles, more challenges and disappointments. I know now that it is in how I cope that will make the difference. Joan Baez is reputed to have said that 'None of us have any control over how or when or where we are going to die; we do have control over how we chose to live.'

25. So am I a spiritual person? One thing I'm positive of, I'm not 'holy'. Going down that road would take a few lifetimes, especially for me. There's another phrase I read some where: 'Religion is for people who are trying their best to stay out of hell. Spirituality is for people who've been there.' Now that sounds more like the road I'm on.

26. I would describe myself as a perfectly ordinary person who was privileged to have an extraordinary experience. I'm glad I shared it. I was blessed and healed, I don't know why. I don't bother probing the depths of theology or philosophy anymore. God has his own plan, and if I follow it as best I can, I'll be okay. 'Turn to me and be safe' (Is 45:22).

27. This is my story and I pray that anyone who reads it will have new hope and a new trust in a God who is always there. Be still, probe the depths of your soul. You won't regret it. I haven't. Hopefully it will make a tiny difference to someone, somewhere. If it does, it was worth writing.